Original title:
Laughing at the Purpose of Life

Copyright © 2025 Creative Arts Management OÜ
All rights reserved.

Author: Harrison Blake
ISBN HARDBACK: 978-1-80566-063-7
ISBN PAPERBACK: 978-1-80566-358-4

Divine Comedy in the Everyday

In the morning rush, we trip and sway,
As coffee turns to laughter, brightening the day.
A sock on the ceiling, a cat in the drawer,
Life's little quirks leave us wanting more.

The toast pops up, a toast to the jest,
We waltz through chaos, life's grand fest.
With giggles at mishaps, we stroll through grace,
Here's to the folly we all must face.

Witty Whims of the Universe

Stars twinkle mischief, a cosmic game,
While planets giggle, 'tis never the same.
A comet sneezes, leaving trails of cheer,
In the play of existence, there's much to hear.

A moonwalk gone wrong, spinning bright,
Gravity chuckles, 'You'll be alright!'
In the vast expanse, we dance and prance,
With whims of the universe leading the chance.

Mirth in the Midst of Meaning

Philosophers ponder in hats rather tall,
While silly little birds fly and squawk with a call.
The depth of our being, weighed in a scale,
Yet a jester appears, making reason derail.

We search for the answers, oh where can they be?
While dogs barter wisdom, invisible glee.
Amidst our deep thoughts, a joke slips on by,
In the heart of this quest, we all laugh and sigh.

Sassy Echoes of the Void

In the emptiness, laughter knows no bounds,
Echoes of sassy jests swirl all around.
Stars wink knowingly, a cosmic tease,
As we chase silly dreams on a cosmic breeze.

The void shouts back with a jest so clear,
'What's life without fun? Just a long career!'
So spin like a top in the great unknown,
With echoes of giggles, we find our throne.

The Punchline of Being

We gather round the cosmic jest,
In every heartbeat, a quirky test.
Life's a stage with oddball roles,
We dance and trip, yet still, we stroll.

The universe chuckles, wide and bright,
With twinkling stars that wink at night.
We juggle dreams like clumsy clowns,
Falling down, yet wearing crowns.

The punchline comes, it makes us sigh,
With every blink, we wonder why.
Yet in our folly, joy ignites,
A riddle wrapped in silly lights.

Tickle My Soul with Paradoxes

In the maze of thoughts, we twist and turn,
Holding lessons we forgot to learn.
Truths and fables tangled tight,
The wrongs feel right under starlit night.

I stagger through with wobbly feet,
Finding wisdom in mischief sweet.
Dancing shadows whisper and tease,
While certainty flutters like a leaf in breeze.

Tickle my soul with paradox jokes,
Life's a puzzle made by jokers' strokes.
We laugh and gasp at what we find,
A world that's silly, yet so kind.

Joyful Nonsense in the Universe

In the grand expanse of the silly sky,
Dancing quarks and giggles fly.
Stars throw parties, and planets spin,
With joyful nonsense wrapped within.

A comet's tail trails laughter bright,
As we chase the absurd through endless night.
Mountains of whimsy, valleys of cheer,
Every echo sings, 'Don't take it near.'

Through cosmic riddles and goofy glee,
We sip the potion of curiosity.
In this chaotic, wondrous scene,
Nonsense reigns, so carefree and keen.

The Grin of Uncertainty

With every step, we fumble and sway,
Uncertainty grins in a cheeky way.
We wear confusion like a crown,
Bouncing back without a frown.

Questions swarm like silly bees,
Life's a riddle, a playful tease.
We skip along this winding path,
Embracing chaos, dodging wrath.

The grin grows wide, the punchlines land,
In this wacky tale, we take a stand.
Finding joy in every twist,
In uncertainty's hug, we can't resist.

The Smirk of Serendipity

Life's a jester in disguise,
With tricks hiding in surprise,
We dance, we trip, we often fall,
Yet somehow, we still stand tall.

Our plans can swirl like autumn leaves,
Woven in webs that fate weaves,
A toast to chaos, cheer, and play,
For who knows what comes our way?

Jests on the Journey

We drive down roads of twists and turns,
Chasing fires that flicker and burn,
A smile brightens the darkest nights,
As we stumble toward our silly sights.

Maps may lie and paths unclear,
Yet every wrong leads us here,
Arm in arm with unexpected glee,
Together we write our history.

Cosmic Chuckles

Stars giggle in their cosmic flight,
Winking bright through the velvet night,
Who would guess on this grand sphere,
That laughter's the music we hold dear?

Planets tumble in a merry race,
While comets paint their silly grace,
What's the point? We dance and spin,
Brighten the chaos that lies within.

Silliness from Stardust

In realms beyond, where dreams collide,
Silliness is our starry guide,
With every twinkle, a giggle's cast,
Reminding us to cherish the vast.

As nights unfold with frolicsome beams,
Fractions of time are fit for dreams,
In a universe of whims, we play,
Crafting joy in our own clumsy way.

Sassy Sagas of the Soul

In the mirror, a wink and a sigh,
Who knew antics could reach for the sky?
With a flip of the hair, a dance in the room,
Life's silly jaunts make boredom just fume.

Dinner plates spin like stars in the night,
We chase our own tails in a comical fight.
A life full of quirks, a joyful parade,
The heart knows a giggle over plans we have laid.

Smirking at Certainty

In a world made of rules, I'll break every mold,
Expect the unexpected, let stories unfold.
With a rollicking grin, let chaos abound,
For certainty's just a laugh that we found.

A roadmap of giggles, a compass of fun,
We dance on the edge where curiosity's spun.
Embrace the unknown with a chuckle and cheer,
For each stumble we make pulls the joy ever near.

The Silly Struggles of Existence

Through tangled routines that twist like a pretzel,
We juggle our dreams, grow weary, and wrestle.
A belly flop splash in the pool of our plight,
Yet the bubbles of laughter keep spirits so bright.

Chasing the minutes like children at play,
The clock winks and giggles, then slips right away.
In chaos we dance, on the whim of our fate,
Finding glee in the madness, it's never too late.

Grins and Gigabytes

Scrolling through life on a digital spree,
Each meme a reminder that we're meant to be free.
Pixels explode like fireworks bright,
In this pixelated world, we laugh to delight.

With a tap, swipe, and scroll we navigate,
Silly pictures flash as we eagerly await.
Connection and humor in data reside,
What's life but a joke we all share with pride?

Chuckling With the Cosmos

Stars twirl in a dance of delight,
Galaxies giggle, what a sight!
Planets wobble in dizzying spins,
While comets gossip about our sins.

Black holes chuckle, pulling us near,
Sucking in dreams, not a hint of fear.
Space is a jester, it's all just play,
We tumble through, come what may.

The Fickle Finger of Fate

Fate winks at us with a twist of a hand,
Stirring the pot, isn't it grand?
We stumble and trip on life's grand stage,
While the universe laughs at our age.

A flip of a coin decides our fate,
Fortune and folly, why contemplate?
In the dance of chance, we twirl and sway,
As laughter echoes, come what may.

Cosmic Capers

Stars play hopscotch on the Milky Way,
Nebulas whisper secrets in dismay.
Jovial giants laugh with glee,
While shooting stars play hide and seek.

Asteroids trip with a comic flair,
Stumbling past Jupiter without a care.
In cosmic mischief, the game unfolds,
A tapestry of humor that never gets old.

Lighthearted Labyrinths

Life's a maze with twists galore,
Each corner hides a jovial score.
We strut through riddles, filled with jest,
In this whirlwind puzzle, we find our best.

A jester's grin in the heart of the path,
Makes every wrong turn a reason for laugh.
Wandering souls on a wild quest,
In lighthearted joy, we find our rest.

Playful Ponderings of the Soul

In a world of plans and schemes,
We stumble on our silly dreams.
With every twist, we find surprise,
The truth is found in silly eyes.

We chase the stars, we miss the train,
And laugh at all our little pain.
The universe just winks at me,
A cosmic dance of glee and glee.

We ponder life's big mystery,
Like solving puzzles, oh what glee!
Each answer blossoms like a flower,
Giggling through our fleeting hour.

Amid the chaos, joy's our guide,
With smiles and laughter side by side.
Let's toss our worries to the wind,
And play until the day's rescind.

Chuckles in the Fabric of Time

Tick-tock the clock, a jest indeed,
As moments flutter, hearts are freed.
We craft our tales, both grand and small,
Yet trip and tumble, through it all.

What's next, a wizard or a clown?
We dance through life, we twirl and frown.
In every twist, a hearty cheer,
For folly is what brought us here.

The past a quilt of laughter bright,
Each stitch a wink of pure delight.
We gather 'round and share our spins,
With hearty hugs and playful grins.

So let's embrace this charming plight,
In every shadow, find the light.
Tomorrow's door, let's leave it ajar,
For joy awaits, just look afar.

The Cosmic Joke

The stars conspire with giggles high,
As planets whirl and comets fly.
We play our parts in this grand show,
Where humor sparkles, watch it glow.

Each question asked, a riddle spun,
In this wild game, we're all just fun.
From serious thoughts, we start to drift,
And find ourselves in laughter's lift.

Oh, universe, with winking eyes,
You tease us gently, oh what lies!
In every stumble, a punchline waits,
As time itself just laughs and tolerates.

So raise a toast to fate's odd schemes,
In burdens light, we chase our dreams.
With every giggle, patterns form,
In cosmic jest, we weather the storm.

Whimsical Whispers of Existence

In a garden where the giggles grow,
We dance around in our silly show.
The sunbeam tickles the morning air,
And whispers secrets without a care.

A butterfly flits, a wink of fate,
In nature's jest, we contemplate.
Each rustle leaves a story bare,
Of life's sweet folly and gentle scare.

Our laughter echoes through the trees,
Like playful whispers on a breeze.
Together we forge a vibrant song,
In this wild web where we belong.

So spin the tales, let spirits soar,
In whimsical ways, forevermore.
The heart reveals what eyes can't see,
A tapestry of joy and glee.

Amusement in the Abyss

In a pit of despair, where shadows collide,
A jester will dance with a grin open wide.
With antics so wild, and a twist of the fate,
We chuckle and ponder, what's life but a mate?

A fish in a suit, on a bicycle rides,
Balancing dreams where absurdity hides.
A cactus donning a top hat and shoes,
Sips tea by the fountain, dismissing the blues.

Revelry Amidst Ruins

In crumbling castles, ghosts share a jest,
They argue in riddles, but still feel so blessed.
A broomstick takes flight, with a cat on the chair,
"Is this where we're headed? Who cares? Let's not care!"

With socks on their heads and shoes on their feet,
They wiggle and giggle, finding life's beat.
In ruins of grandeur, there's laughter and cheer,
For time's just a trick, and we're all still here.

The Funny Side of Forever

Eternity's a trip with no map or guide,
You'll find a parade with a duck as the slide.
It quacks out the secrets of time bending wise,
While laughter erupts when a snail starts to rise.

We stroll through the fabric of moments and beams,
Each tick is a tickle, a burst of wild dreams.
In a universe spinning, absurd and bright,
The purpose is silly, all dressed up in light.

Cackles in the Cosmic Flow

A comet scoffs loud as it whizzes on by,
Throwing cosmic confetti and stardust to fly.
A space octopus juggles the planets with glee,
While aliens dance, sipping tea by the sea.

In a realm of the bizarre, time's lost in delight,
Each moment's a giggle that shines through the night.
So join in the revels of this odd cosmic show,
Where laughter and nonsense in tandem will flow.

The Game of Cosmic Quirk

In the grand circus of fate, we jest,
Where chaos dons a jester's vest.
Stars giggle in their twinkling play,
As we trip on this life, come what may.

Questions dart like fireflies bright,
While answers hide in the dark of night.
With each twist, we twirl and sway,
What's serious here? Let's toss it away.

The moon winks from its silver throne,
As we dance with the unknown, alone.
The universe grins, a cheeky sprite,
Inviting us to join the delight.

So here's our dance, a fabulous jest,
Life's riddle is best left unguessed.
With a bounce, a hop, and a cheer,
Let's spin in this absurd frontier.

Whirlwinds of Laughter

In fields of whimsy, ideas sprout,
Where giggles churn in a wild rout.
The clouds wear hats, fluffy and bright,
As we wander in this curious light.

Wobbly thoughts like jellybeans flow,
Tickling the mind in a vibrant show.
Rain drops tap in a silly song,
Each splash a jest as we dance along.

The sun cracks jokes with rays of glee,
Inviting all to join in the spree.
Stars chime in, a chorus so sweet,
Celebrating life with whimsical beats.

With every turn, a chuckle grows,
As the universe spins in giggling throes.
Embrace the whirl, let laughter sail,
For the joy of it all is rich without fail.

A Smirk in Every Corner

Peeking through time's sly little grin,
Life reveals where the fun begins.
In every shadow, a giggle hides,
Turning the tides where mischief bides.

A wink from the cat in the tree,
Cosmic jokes shared with glee.
Step on a crack and the universe winks,
Provoking thoughts and vibrant blinks.

In bustling streets, the humor's vast,
As moments blend, both slow and fast.
Every corner holds a playful tale,
Of silly things that never grow pale.

With a chuckle here and a grin so wide,
We walk the path of absurd pride.
So let us frolic through our days,
Chasing smirks in hilarious ways.

Playful Parables of the Universe

Once upon a cosmic lore,
A dance unfolded, never a bore.
Planets played tag, stars skipped around,
In this tale of whimsy, joy abounds.

Each comet's tail tells a joke so sly,
As galaxies chuckle and whirl by.
Life's fables twist with mischief's glee,
In the grand story, we're wild and free.

Quirky moments float like balloons,
Filling the air with playful tunes.
Adventures await in laughter's embrace,
In the universe's heart, we find our place.

So gather round, let's share the fun,
For every heart beats as one.
In this playful parable we call life,
Laughter dances, banishing strife.

Laughter in the Face of Fate

In a world where plans go awry,
We wear our whims like a tie.
Juggling dreams, some fall to the ground,
Yet in their tumble, joy is found.

Mirrors crack with every jest,
Reflections show what we like best.
A wink at fate, a playful nudge,
Why not dance, instead of judge?

Fate's a prankster, a quirky mate,
With twists and turns, like a wild date.
We stumble, giggle, roll on the floor,
Life's absurdity opens the door.

So here we are, with chuckles as crowns,
In silly hats and mismatched gowns.
With every mishap, we take a bow,
Life's a jest, and oh, here and now!

A Playful Dance with Reality

Reality winks, a whimsical dance,
Steps are wrong but give it a chance.
With every trip over stray feet,
Life's a tune that catches the beat.

Swirling in circles, we twirl and glide,
A partner in chaos, let's enjoy the ride.
The music plays, off-key but loud,
We laugh at the slips, oh, aren't we proud?

The world spins wild in vibrant hues,
We're the jesters, wearing our shoes.
In shadows of reason, we prance and slide,
What's serious now? None can decide.

So here we spin, in joyful delight,
In a playful dance that feels so right.
Each stumble's a burst of sparkly cheer,
Embracing the crazy, we persevere!

Riddles Wrapped in Paradox

Questions circle like buzzing flies,
Truths are hidden, wrapped in disguise.
The answers giggle, darting away,
Who really knows at the end of the day?

In laughter we search for what is real,
Is it folly, or is this the deal?
We juggle puzzles, quite absurd,
In the chaos, joy is stirred.

Wrapped in riddles, dressed so fine,
The essence of life is a puzzling line.
We scratch our heads, our spirits soar,
The more we ponder, the less we score.

Yet in the mystery, we find our song,
With every twist, we feel we belong.
So let's embrace the paradox anew,
With giggles that bind me and you!

The Humor Hidden in Chaos

Amidst the turmoil, a chuckle brews,
In frantic moments, nothing is true.
The clock runs backwards, birds wear shoes,
In this madness, how could we lose?

A puzzle box with no clear key,
We fumble, we trip, lost at sea.
But in the whirl, a joke unfolds,
A ticket to mirth, excitement, and gold.

Chaos a canvas, so messy and bright,
Each splash of laughter becomes our light.
We twirl through the fragments, a playful spree,
Finding humor where none should be.

So let's toast the mishaps, the circus we share,
With laughter that's light, floating in air.
In the chaos, we dance and we sing,
For in the absurd, joy takes wing!

Giggles in the Grand Design

In a world where socks go missing,
Toasters burn just out of spite,
A cat will steal your morning,
And laugh at your sleepy plight.

The sun seems to rise just for fun,
While we chase our tails like fools,
The clock ticks slow, then races ahead,
As we try to stick to the rules.

Balloons float high, dreams drift away,
Logic wears a silly hat,
We're scholars of whimsy, on this odd stage,
Debating why the chicken crossed that mat.

So here's to the chaos, the jests divine,
A dance with whimsy, a sweet redesign,
Each stumble a chance, each fumble a glee,
In this grand design, we spin carefree.

Witty Echoes in the Void

In the void where stardust plays,
Echoes of laughter softly ring,
Why worry about the big 'why not?'
When the moon itself loves to sing.

Clouds giggle softly when they rain,
They swipe at dreams with a playful air,
While aliens sip on stellar tea,
And wink at us with cosmic flair.

Time trips over its own shoelace,
As we pile up questions like witless fools,
Yet wisdom often wears mismatched socks,
Who needs a map when you've got tools?

So throw your worries up with the stars,
Let them dance on Milky Way beams,
For life is a stage, a merry charade,
Filled with odd, hilarious dreams.

The Irony of Our Journey

We travel the roads of fortune's jest,
With mishaps as our best friends,
Maps lead us nowhere, yet we insist,
On finding where the fun bends.

The paths we tread are riddled with glee,
A wise man's folly, a fool's delight,
Every wrong turn a story unfolds,
Bringing laughter to the night.

We quest for reason in a sea of surprise,
Knights wielding plunger swords,
Searching for wisdom in cereal boxes,
In this game without any chords.

Oh irony, you sly little sprite,
You tickle our minds in absurdity's tide,
With giggles echoing our folly-filled plight,
As we dance through the mystery we abide.

Smiles Beneath the Stars

Beneath the stars, we spread our dreams,
With comets painting silly scenes,
A toast to chaos, a wink from fate,
In cosmic jest, we navigate.

Constellations laugh as we stumble along,
In our quest for meaning, a whimsical song,
A jester's cap upon the moon's face,
Giggles echo in empty space.

We ponder the vastness with playful grins,
As gravity pulls at our sides' whims,
With every twirl, we celebrate,
The humor hidden in life's great fate.

So here's to the moments, both ridiculous and bright,
When laughter fills the dark of night,
With every heartbeat, let joy ignite,
As we smile beneath the stars' soft light.

The Cheerful Chaos Parade

In a world where puddles gleam,
Silly hats and ice cream streams,
Dancing ducks in polka dots,
Life's a joke that never stops.

Balloons that float and giggle high,
Ticklish clouds, a painted sky,
Whimsical tunes in the air,
Laughter bubbles everywhere.

Jesters juggle, making mess,
Wobbling thoughts, a joyful stress,
Chasing squirrels with bright balloons,
Life's a stage with quirky tunes.

Stepping stones in clownish shoes,
Giggling past the morning blues,
In the chaos, take a seat,
Join the parade, feel the beat.

Smiles in the Shadows

In corners dark where chuckles dwell,
Whispers tease and giggles swell,
Shadows dance with jolly glee,
Life's a riddle, wild and free.

Twirling tales like cotton candy,
Serious faces? Oh, too dandy!
We crawl beneath the frowning sun,
Find the joy, the silly fun.

Fingers pointing at the moon,
Swirling thoughts in a silly tune,
Laughter echoes in the night,
Silliness brings the world delight.

Tiptoe past the troubled minds,
Where in a chuckle, peace one finds,
A secret vault of smiles bright,
In shadows, bask in pure delight.

Ecstatic Anarchy of Being

Here we stand in a messy pile,
Witty grins that stretch a mile,
Stumbles turn to daring leaps,
Life's a dance that never sleeps.

Balancing on a crooked line,
Jokes that mix with each sip of wine,
Reality bends with a smirk,
In our folly, we find great work.

Chasing whims like butterflies,
Silly truths in our alibis,
Every misstep, quite the thrill,
Life's an art—unpainted still.

Tangled laughs, we break the norm,
From chaos, art begins to form,
So let's skewer serious fate,
And celebrate this wondrous state.

Quirky Reflections

Mirror games in wild disguise,
Nonsense giggles, truth in lies,
Reflections twist, a comedy,
Making merry of gravity.

Bouncing thoughts with rubber shoes,
Kooky dreams we love to choose,
Glimpses of the weird and wild,
In each misstep, we're all a child.

Chasing shadows, catch a grin,
Life's a riddle — let's begin,
Throw the map away and roam,
Find the joy in every foam.

Through quirky paths, we skip and shout,
There's freedom in the funny route,
With every turn, let laughter reign,
In this dance, we'll feel no pain.

Puns on the Path of Life

In the garden of fate, we see the signs,
With every step, we dance on the lines.
Tripping on fate, with grins wide and bright,
Life's a maze, oh what a sight!

We juggle dreams like hot potato,
With wishes flying, a crazy tornado.
Stumbling through plans, we giggle and cheer,
What was the point? Oh dear, oh dear!

With puns in our pockets, we wander and roam,
Each twist a giggle, like finding a home.
A slippery slope, a comedic slide,
On this path, we take life in stride.

So here's to the puns that keep us alive,
In this grand circus where zaniness thrives.
Each quip a treasure, we gather with glee,
Life's a pun, come laugh along with me!

Nutty Narratives of Nature

The squirrel on a branch mocks the wise old tree,
With acorns aplenty, as smug as can be.
He spins tales of grandeur, a nutty charade,
While the leaves just rustle, amused and dismayed.

The sun peeks in, a playful old friend,
Stirring the shadows, making daylight bend.
A flower giggles, it sways with the breeze,
While a bee buzzes loudly with comical ease.

In this circus of creatures, all jesters abound,
A parade of oddities, joy's glory found.
As nature recounts its curious lore,
We chuckle and grin, always wanting more.

So chase after stories, let humor ignite,
In the nutty embrace of a whimsical night.
Nature's a banquet of laughter and cheer,
A narrative rich, forever held dear!

When Life Plays Tricks

A jester named Time, with a wink in his eye,
Pulls pranks on our plans, oh my, oh my!
Turning day into night with a flick of his wand,
We chase after dreams, but they simply abscond.

A mirror reflects what we wish to deny,
With every reflection, our hopes fly awry.
Like clowns in a circus, we slip and we fall,
Yet the laughter that echoes is the best gift of all.

We juggle our worries, they bounce and they roll,
Each slip of the heart, a punchline, a goal.
When life plays its tricks, we smile through the haze,
For in folly and fun, we find our best days.

So let's tip our hats to the mischief afoot,
For the jesters of life keep us light on our foot.
In every twist taken, there's joy to unearth,
When life plays its tricks, it's the best kind of mirth!

Amusing Antics of Existence

Existence is a dance, a pirouette, a spin,
Where the stage is a world, we all jump in.
We trip on our thoughts, like clowns in a show,
Each mishap a punchline, as laughter will flow.

In the carnival of choices, we toss and we turn,
With whims in abundance, there's so much to learn.
A jest from the universe, a wink from the stars,
Guides us through life, with all of its bars.

Like silly balloons, we float and collide,
In this goofy parade, we take life in stride.
With antics aplenty and whimsy our muse,
We relish the chaos, nothing to lose.

So come join the fun, let your worries set free,
In this amusing absurdity, so wild, so glee.
For existence is laughter, a goofy delight,
In the grand circus of life, we star every night!

Smirking at the Spiral of Life

Twists and turns in the grand old ride,
We twirl like tops, with no place to hide.
Questions hang like fruit from trees,
But gravity pulls us with gentle ease.

Socks mismatched, a puzzle undone,
Dancing in circles, we're just having fun.
The map is scribbles, the path unclear,
Yet we skip along, with nothing to fear.

Time ticks slowly, then races ahead,
Bumping into dreams we never had.
A wink from the cosmos, a friendly nudge,
Reminding us all not to take the grudge.

Eternal jesters in a cosmic play,
Each pratfall and slip makes bright our day.
So grab a giggle, life's just a game,
With joy in our hearts, we stay ever the same.

The Farce of Fate's Design

A plot thick with twists, a comedy arc,
Life's great script is a walk in the park.
Tripping on shoelaces, we tumble and fall,
Yet with every mishap, we stand proud and tall.

The stage is set in an awkward light,
With punchlines galore that take flight.
We wear our costumes, mismatched and bold,
In the circus of life, the tales are retold.

The punch and the jab, life's playful tease,
Each moment we savor, like a warm summer breeze.
With hats on our heads and smiles on our face,
We dance through the chaos, embracing the pace.

A slapstick serenade, a comedic flow,
In the grand show of life, we steal the show.
So join the encore, let laughter arise,
For in this farce, we find our prize.

Reveling in Ridiculous Realities

Coffee spills and shoe untied,
In the merry mishaps, we take pride.
Tickling fancies and odd little quirks,
Life's a circus; we're the happy jerks.

Each mishap's a joke that's begging to land,
Juggling our fates with a clumsy hand.
The clock might mock with its ticking sound,
Yet we laugh at the chaos that's all around.

Bouncing through puddles, we splash with style,
Embracing each hiccup, mile after mile.
With a heart full of glee and a grin ear to ear,
We toast to the shenanigans, year after year.

So gather your friends for a wacky show,
In this grand tale, we're all in the know.
Let's revel in silliness, dance in delight,
For life's absurdity makes everything bright.

The Satirical Symphony of Being

In the symphony of chaos, we play our notes,
With rhythms of laughter in quirky boats.
The conductor grins with a stick made of fluff,
As we pirouette through the silly and tough.

Harmony found in the oddest of ways,
Chasing our dreams through the whimsical haze.
With comic relief and a wink to the crowd,
We leap and we twirl, joyous and loud.

The dance of existence, a flick of the wrist,
In this madcap ballet, we can't resist.
So who's got the tune? We hum and we sway,
In this grand concert of folly, we play.

So follow the laughter; it leads to the cheer,
In the symphony of life, the joy's always near.
With a chorus of giggles, we take our stance,
In the theater of being, come join the dance!

The Outrageous Odyssey

In the quest for wisdom's gold,
We stumble, giggle, and feel bold.
Chasing dreams that swiftly fade,
We find a joke in every trade.

With maps drawn freehand, circles wide,
We navigate with hearts that glide.
Missteps become our guiding stars,
Each blunder takes us near and far.

We dance through fields of silly plans,
While time slips through our clumsy hands.
Heroes of a timeless tale,
With laughter, always we set sail.

The universe winks in its madness,
Flinging chaos in playful gladness.
Through every twist, bizarre and bright,
We chuckle softly into the night.

Grinning in the Granularity

In the tiny pixels of our plight,
We find the quirks that spark delight.
Every moment, a chuckle, a smile,
Life's absurdities stretch a mile.

We dress our frowns in vibrant hues,
As cosmic clowns, we heal our blues.
Each near stumble, a fateful slip,
Turns into a joyful trip.

Sandcastles built on shifting sand,
With waves that laugh at our grand plan.
Yet, in the froth and foam we see,
The humor baked in the history.

So we toast to folly, raise a cheer,
For every gaffe we hold so dear.
In this grand dance of joy and jest,
We find the truth within the jest.

Folly in the Fabric of Life

Stitch by stitch, we weave our tale,
With threads of mishaps, bold and frail.
A tapestry of blunders bright,
Each frayed end brings pure delight.

We trip on paths of twisted lace,
Yet bump into a warm embrace.
Every wrong turn shows us grace,
In the unexpected, we find our place.

With needle pricks that gather cheer,
We thread the needle without fear.
While logic fades in wide-eyed glee,
We stitch together absurdity.

So here we stand, with fabric torn,
In patches worn, from laughter born.
Life's confusion, always rife,
Is but a quilt of joyful strife.

The Jest of Existence

In the grand play where jesters stride,
We slip on happiness, our guide.
Each line delivered with flair and zest,
Turns mundane times into a fest.

We juggle worries in a mix,
With humor's charm, we find our kicks.
A twist of fate, a cosmic joke,
We share a laugh, the world awoke.

Like butterflies in a twirling breeze,
We land ungraceful, with such ease.
Our smiles bloom like flowers bright,
In life's theater, we find our light.

So take a bow, embrace the farce,
For every moment, we'll hold and parse.
In this jest, our hearts reside,
Finding joy wherever we glide.

Lurid Laughter of the Universe

When stars twinkle with glee,
And planets waltz in wobbly spins,
Comets giggle as they flee,
While black holes wear their silly grins.

Eons pass in a cosmic joke,
Time stretches on, what a lark!
Galaxies whisper and poke,
As they twirl in the dark.

Each quasar beams a cheeky wink,
Every meteor a playful tease,
As they dance, they barely think,
Just swirling in the cosmic breeze.

So next time you gaze at the night,
Remember the universe plays, you see,
In its grand, luminous light,
There's humor in all there will be.

Absurd Audacity

In a world where cats reign supreme,
And dogs compose their barks in verse,
Fish swim quietly, plotting a scheme,
While plants argue who's better, terse.

The chairs hold meetings on who should sit,
While shoes conspire to run away,
And spoons chatter, refusing to quit,
As the forks come out to play.

Each day unfolds in splendid whim,
With life's circus marching bold,
Tickling truths just on a limb,
As the stories of nonsense unfold.

So raise a glass to the absurd show,
To cheers of a life unplanned,
For in folly, we blissfully flow,
Searching for fun, hand in hand.

The Gleeful Glimpse Beyond

Peeking through a crack in fate,
Strange wonders always greet the eye,
With giggles of life, we celebrate,
As moments pass, oh my, oh my!

The wind whispers its playful tease,
Telling tales of the sun's sly grin,
Clouds decorate with joyful ease,
As the rain dances, joyfully thin.

Each stumble on the path of dreams,
A nudge from clumsy cosmic sprites,
Life's not always as it seems,
Yet silliness colors our nights.

Raise a toast to the wild ride,
To the quirks that make us grin,
For in the chaos, fun does abide,
As we spin in this charming spin.

Sassy Snickers from the Skies

When thunder rumbles with a chuckle,
And lightning winks through the haze,
The clouds begin to softly snuggle,
In a stormy dance, such a craze.

Raindrops fall like tiny jokes,
Each splash a gentle, sassy slap,
While puddles gather, sharing pokes,
In nature's light-hearted trap.

Up above, the sun waves bright,
Winking through the rainy spree,
Its glow brings laughter, pure delight,
As it beams down, carefree as can be.

So listen close, as the skies sing,
With humor drizzled on our face,
For in this life, it's a joyful fling,
Finding cheer in every space.

Revelations Wrapped in Jest

In a world spun wild with glee,
Clowns wear masks for all to see.
Truths parade in a quirky dance,
Life's a jest, a well-timed chance.

With every slip, we giggle loud,
Dancing under a joke-filled cloud.
The wise may frown, but we just grin,
In our folly, we all win.

Each mishap's just a place to start,
Tickling our ever-busy heart.
For every question, there's a pun,
In this circus, we have our fun.

So raise a glass to life's fair game,
In the humor, we find our fame.
With laughter's echo, we embark,
On paths where shadows leave their mark.

The Absurdity of Our Play

Jesters prance in colors bright,
While wisdom hides from the limelight.
In every quip and silly tease,
Life's a riddle with no keys.

We juggle dreams like rubber balls,
And stumble through these hallowed halls.
Questions float on a feathered breeze,
Who needs answers when we can tease?

Each blunder paints a masterpiece,
Crafted in moments of playful fleece.
So let us dance, let spirits sway,
In the absurdity of our play.

With every laugh, the world grows wide,
Inviting us on this joyful ride.
Embrace the odd, the upside-down,
In our hearts, we wear the crown.

Humorous Horizons of the Heart

When time tick-tocks with a grin,
Life's a game where jokes begin.
Chasing dreams on a bouncing spree,
What is real? Oh, who can see?

With whims and giggles in the air,
We build our castles without care.
Every moment's a playful prank,
With laughter soaring, spirits dank.

We paint the sky with a giddy hue,
Each mishap brings a laugh anew.
If purpose hides, let laughter reign,
In our folly, we find the gain.

So open wide those joyous gates,
Forget the cares, embrace the fates.
For in this dance of hearts so free,
Humor's horizon is all we see.

Silly Shadows in the Light of Existence

Beneath the sun, shadows prance,
In their silliness, take a chance.
Life's a circus, no need to stress,
With each blunder, we love the mess.

Silly hats and mismatched shoes,
We play our part, we simply choose.
Every fumble, a comedy sketch,
With laughs to soothe, we'll find our catch.

In this theater of grand design,
The punchlines land, like aged wine.
So giggle loudly, let spirits lift,
For smiles, my friend, are the greatest gift.

Embrace the quirks, the bizarre sight,
In the shadows, we find delight.
For life's a jest, with no regret,
In silly shadows, we laugh, we met.

The Jester's Dance of Destiny

In a world where clowns wear crowns,
The jester prances in silly gowns.
With every step, a chuckle flies,
As fate wears goggles and a comical disguise.

Gags and pratfalls light the way,
Through twists of fate, we laugh and play.
A pie in the face, a dance so bold,
Reveals the secrets life's tales hold.

A tumble here, a slide in jest,
We trip through life, ignoring the quest.
For every stumble brings a grin,
In this merry world where fun begins.

So grab a horn, let laughter ring,
In the circus of life, we're all the king.
Each punchline rolls like waves to shore,
In the jester's dance, who could want more?

Whispers of Cosmic Chuckles

Stars giggle in the vast night sky,
As planets waltz with a wink and a sigh.
Galaxies swirl in a playful jest,
In the universe's heart, we're all a quest.

Comets dash with a sparkling grin,
While suns burst forth with a warm, bright spin.
Life's a riddle wrapped in a rhyme,
With each silly clue, we're biding our time.

Nebulas puff as if they share jokes,
Eluding the wisdom of wise stargazers' cloaks.
In the cosmic dance, we twirl and sway,
Chasing stardust and laughter's play.

So listen closely, hear it unfold,
The whispers of stars, a story retold.
For in the laughter of the night so deep,
Life's greatest secrets are ours to keep.

Grinning Through the Abyss

In shadows deep, we find our light,
With smiles so wide, we banish the fright.
The void may rumble, but we giggle back,
In the cosmic joke, we uncover the knack.

A dance on the edge of the unknown,
Where folly blooms and fear's overthrown.
With roars of laughter, we face the dark,
Lighting the way like a playful spark.

The abyss may roar, but we strike a pose,
Dressed in humor, in mismatched clothes.
With wit as our sword and joy as our shield,
Together we conquer the fate that is sealed.

So here's to the journey, the twist and the turn,
In life's grand stage, we forever learn.
Through giggles and grins, we'll never miss,
For even in darkness, there's boundless bliss.

The Comedian's Guide to Existence

In the comedy club of life's great show,
With jokes in hand, we steal the flow.
Each punchline paves a path so bright,
Turning the mundane into sheer delight.

Observations sharp like a stand-up's wit,
Make light of troubles, never to quit.
With laughter's embrace, we share the stage,
And navigate life's silly little page.

Every mishap is a setup for cheer,
The more absurd, the more we endear.
So raise a toast to life's playful prose,
In this zany script, anything goes!

So take a seat, let's chuckle along,
In this magnificent absurdity, we belong.
For in the laughter, the truth is revealed,
The comedian's guide is forever concealed.

Witty Whims of the Wanderer

In a world where socks mispair,
And dreams float like a feather in air,
I stroll on clouds made of candy floss,
Chasing giggles, ignoring the loss.

Every step's a question, a riddle, a tease,
Why not dance with fate, do as you please?
Life's a circus, just popcorn and flair,
With clowns playing chess, unaware of despair.

I wonder, do clouds wear hats in disguise?
Do rainbows blush when they kiss the skies?
Nah, they just chuckle and float on a breeze,
While we chase our tails, hoping for ease.

So here's to the whimsy, the silly and sweet,
To the joys of the journey, not just the feat.
As we trip over cobblestones, giggles unfold,
With every misstep, life's secrets are told.

The Cheeky Chronicles of Chaos

A fruitcake's ambition, so bold yet absurd,
Dreaming of being a soft, fluffy bird.
While socks hold a summit, discussing their fate,
And spoons tell the forks they're never too late.

Mustard and ketchup engage in a spat,
Over who's the best condiment, witty and fat.
Yet fries roll their eyes, with a crisp little grin,
Knowing their crunch always lets them win.

The pillows plot schemes to keep us awake,
While blankets conspire to take a long break.
And time wears a watch that runs fashionably late,
Making minutes dance, oh isn't it great?

Here's to the chaos, the joy that's within,
To the pranks life plays, and the laughter we spin.
For in this madcap world, we find our delight,
In each quirky tale, in the day and the night.

Buffoonery in the Balance

A cat wears a tie, oh what a delight,
While dogs toss confetti, celebrating the night.
With fish playing poker, what a bizarre sight,
Life flips its cards, and we're caught up tight.

The moon's winking down with a playful grin,
While stars snicker softly, encouraging sin.
And gravity giggles as we stumble and fall,
Balancing dreams on the edge of a brawl.

In this jester's parade, where laughter takes wing,
Chaos becomes art, a whimsical fling.
So bring out the banter, the chuckles divine,
For life's but a stage, and we're writing the line.

Embrace the absurdity, dance on the beam,
With humor our lantern, we'll follow the dream.
As long as we're laughing, with joy in our glance,
Life's just a game, so let's take a chance.

Playful Provocations of Existence

A tadpole writes poetry, so clever and sly,
While the wise owl hoots, asking why oh why?
Then bees start debating the best type of flower,
In a world that's a stage, life finds its power.

The sun wears pajamas, lazing through noon,
While the clouds throw a party under the moon.
With crickets as DJs, creating a scene,
Life puts on a show, just to keep it serene.

What if chairs could talk, with stories to share?
Or pencils could giggle, as they sketch in thin air?
The ink flows with mischief, the paper a mime,
In this playful existence, there's no sense of time.

So here's to the smiles, the quirks on our path,
To the laughter that echoes, a joyful aftermath.
For in this grand chaos, we twirl and we sway,
Embracing the nonsense in our own silly way.

Tickled by Fate's Quirks

In the jester's cap, a riddle lies,
Fate dances clumsily, what a surprise!
The world spins round like a child's top,
With giggles galore, we just can't stop.

A banana peel, a cosmic slide,
We stumble forward with eyes open wide.
Life serves us punchlines wrapped in glee,
Who knew mischief had a degree?

The cat'll pounce, the dog will bark,
A trip and a tumble; it's all a lark.
We toast to randomness, raise a glass,
With every twist, we eagerly laugh.

Every question posed, a joke unfolds,
Reality's script is filled with gold.
In the comedy club of stars above,
We find our joy, and that's enough!

Ridiculous Reveries of the Cosmos

Galaxies giggle in the vast unknown,
Silly asteroids play fetch with the moon.
Stars wear wigs and dance a jig,
While planets wobble in a cosmic gig.

Comets sneeze, and meteors trail,
A celestial circus, complete with a whale.
Puppy stars bark at their own tails,
In this grand play, humor prevails.

Black holes burp with a thunderous sound,
As supernovas pop like confetti around.
Time ticks funny; it's all a joke,
Cosmic comedians, wide-eyed and woke.

So ponder away on your tiny sphere,
In the universe, there's nothing to fear.
For every question with weight you possess,
Comes a punchline wrapped up in jest!

Jokes Scribbled on the Canvas of Time

Time's a painter with a messy brush,
Doodling laughs in a timeless rush.
Moments giggle as they race by,
Painting mishaps as we comply.

Calendar jokes on every page,
Each new day brings a slapstick stage.
Witty whispers in the quiet night,
Turn shadowy fears into sheer delight.

Yesterday fumbles, tomorrow's a hoot,
As today dances in a funny suit.
Historic blunders, we celebrate loud,
In this memory-filled, joyous crowd.

Ink on the paper, it tends to sway,
Reminding us to laugh through the fray.
Life's a sketch with a twist and a pun,
A masterpiece crafted, oh what fun!

Sarcastic Stardust and Celestial Humor

Stardust whispers witty lines,
As planets plot their next designs.
Gravity slips on a cosmic shoe,
With every misstep, the universe coos.

Sarcastic beams shine down from above,
Mocking our worries, showing their love.
Meteor showers like confetti rain,
In this absurd cosmic game.

Asteroids chuckle, colliding with fate,
Making friends where they once were late.
Jupiter grins, and Saturn rolls eyes,
As the vastness spins into joyous skies.

So take a cue from the galaxies wide,
Embrace the absurd; come take a ride.
For life's a jest, a tale spun anew,
In a universe where laughter is true!

Pranks of the Infinite

In the cosmic dance, we trip and fall,
Gravity's a joke, we can't stand tall.
Stars wink at us, oh what a sight,
Time's a trickster, playing all night.

Fate throws pies, oh what a mess,
We wear cream smiles, feeling blessed.
Plans we make vanish like smoke,
Life tells us jokes we can't provoke.

A cosmic giggle, the universe sways,
We chase our tails in a blushing haze.
Every heartbeat, a punchline found,
In this grand prank show, we're laughter-bound.

So here's to the jesters, forever bold,
Dancing through ages, stories retold.
Let's join the fun, in endless jest,
In the grand scheme, we're all just blessed.

Jovial Journeys through Time

Time travels quickly, like a sprightly hare,
Waving at moments, it doesn't care.
Yesterday's trouble, just a silly rhyme,
Giggling with joy—oh, the sweetness of time!

We hop through eras, boots on our feet,
Dancing with history, a whimsical feat.
Sailing on laughter, we ride the waves,
In a boat made of jokes—oh, how it braves!

Every tick of the clock, a riddle laid bare,
Making us ponder, while fixing our hair.
With giggles of wisdom, the ancients confide,
Life's not about rules, but a merry ride.

So gather your friends, let's travel the past,
In search of the chuckles, and moments to last.
We're voyagers of joy, not bound by the grind,
In a time-tickle loop, let's unwind.

The Ticklish Tapestry of Life

Life weaves its threads with a cheeky grin,
Frolicking patterns where mischief begins.
We tug at the seams, and what do we find?
A belly full of laughter, wildly unlined.

Each day a thread, colors bright and bold,
Stitched with the antics we dare to unfold.
Life's a fabric, fun and slightly askew,
With patches of whimsy, and moments anew.

Through giggles and gaffes, the stitches hold tight,
Whirling us 'round in a tapestry light.
With every mishap, a smile surely awaits,
In this patchwork of joy, open the gates.

So grab the loom, let's weave and we'll play,
With each poke and nudge, we'll brighten the day.
Life's ticklish dishpay, a blanket of cheer,
In this vibrant quilt, we've nothing to fear.

Mischief in the Mirror

Glimpses of giggles in the glassy sheen,
Reflections dancing, oh what a scene!
Our faces twist in playful surprise,
Mischief abounds behind curious eyes.

Embrace the quirk, the jester within,
With every blunder, let laughter begin.
The mirror chuckles, as we pose and play,
Mimicking life in a comical way.

Shadows tell stories of quirks and delight,
Painting our flaws in the soft moonlight.
With every glance, a blend of absurd,
Life's silly poetry—oh how we've stirred!

So here's to the mirrors, reflecting our fun,
Creating a canvas where humor runs.
In this gallery of pose, let's be absurd,
In the mischief of kin, let our joy be heard.

Tickling Destiny's Fancy

In a world where socks go stray,
And spoons refuse to play,
We dance in circles, oh so bright,
Chasing shadows through the night.

With coffee cups that spill and slide,
And plans that often take a ride,
We find our way, quite unaware,
Of life's grand scheme, a dizzying affair.

The sun's a comedian, bold and loud,
Tickling clouds, drawing a crowd,
While we just giggle, jest and prance,
As we twirl in a foolish dance.

In every stumble, every twist,
A punchline waits, so hard to resist,
Embracing chaos, a cheerful spree,
In this ticklish waltz of irony.

The Absurdity of Being Here

Why do we wander, lost and free,
In quests for answers, can't you see?
With each misstep, we can't quite care,
About the reason we are here.

Life's a parade of wacky sights,
Worms in coats, and ants in tights,
As purpose hides behind a door,
We giggle at what's in store.

The cats debate just what it means,
To chase the light or nibble greens,
While clocks tick on, and birds do sing,
We marvel at the quirky thing.

In the kitchen, pots have a chat,
About where that lost sock sat,
We shrug and smile, take a cheer,
To the madness that brought us here.

Jests of the Universe

Stars wink down with a cheeky glare,
As planets spin without a care,
In a cosmos bursting at the seams,
We chase the wildest of our dreams.

Comets skate on a cosmic stage,
While satellites scribble in a rage,
Each quark and lepton has its jest,
In the grand game, we're just a pest.

Birds pass notes in feathered flight,
Sharing giggles as day turns night,
Fish in water laugh with glee,
At the folly of you and me.

So here we play, in vast expanse,
Joining the universe's dance,
With every chuckle, spin, and twirl,
We find our joy in this absurd swirl.

Chuckles Beneath the Stars

Under a sky of twinkling light,
Where dreams are born in pure delight,
We lay and ponder, oh so free,
The jokes the universe makes of me.

Constellations giggle, making plans,
As meteors streak and dance like fans,
While we fumble for the right reply,
To cosmic questions drifting by.

With every sunset, another pun,
Life's silly lessons have just begun,
We share a laugh with each new dawn,
As if to say, just carry on!

So let's embrace this foolish jest,
In the chaos, we are blessed,
Beneath the stars, so full of glee,
We find the laughter, you and me.

The Comedy of Cosmic Timing

Stars twinkle in a cosmic play,
Tick-tock, the universe in disarray.
Planets spin with a reckless charm,
While comets wink, causing no alarm.

Galaxies dance in a ragged line,
Time's the punchline, everything's fine.
Wormholes whisper with a cosmic jest,
Who knows if we're just a fest of the blessed?

In a moment of light years, we all collide,
Infinity grins, no need to hide.
With each quirk of fate, a giggle emerges,
In this grand scheme, absurdity surges.

Finding Fun in the Fractals

Patterns swirl in a dizzying spree,
Life's a fractal, wild and free.
Zoom in tight on each winking face,
Each tiny moment in a cosmic race.

Laughter echoes in every line,
Swirls and curls do a funny design.
Chaos dances with perfect grace,
In this odd world, there's a laugh to embrace.

The simple and complex smile hand in hand,
In this paradox, let humor stand.
Life's a puzzle, a riddle in jest,
Finding joy in the chaotic quest.

Laughs Lurking in Life's Labyrinth

A maze of dreams and whimsical turns,
Each corner holds a laugh that burns.
Down winding paths, we stumble and clash,
Falling face-first—oh, what a splash!

Questions dance in shadows and light,
Life's absurdities bring pure delight.
The exit's a joke, a mirage unseen,
Yet the fun's in the chase, all in between.

Witty signs point nowhere at all,
With each wrong turn, we stumble and fall.
Nonsense reigns in this joyful spree,
Who knew confusion could set us free?

The Amusement of Existence

Life's a carnival, bright and loud,
With ups and downs, we're part of the crowd.
Spinning rides make our heads whirl,
As laughter spreads like a joyful pearl.

Clowns in big shoes, a humorous sight,
Juvenile giggles that dance in the night.
Each moment's a ticket, a humorous game,
Stepping through life, it's never the same.

Balloons float high, dreams in the sky,
While silly thoughts make us ponder why.
The fair never ends, it's an endless spree,
In this joyous circus, oh, let us be free.

The Funnies of Fate

Life's a jester in a cap,
With tricks that make us clap.
A dance of chance in every turn,
In folly's grasp, we twist and yearn.

The clock just laughs, it won't slow down,
As we chase dreams in a paper crown.
We're all on stage, it's quite absurd,
With lines forgotten, and yet unheard.

Through twists and turns, we slip and slide,
A merry-go-round we can't abide.
Yet here we are with smiles so wide,
In this circus where clowns reside.

Each stumble brings a hearty cheer,
A cosmic joke that's crystal clear.
Though purpose hides in shadows gray,
We prance along, come what may.

Jocular Jaunts of Existence

Waking up is quite the show,
With dishes flying to and fro.
Coffee spills while the cat takes flight,
We dance through chaos, hearts so light.

The universe spins with a grin,
As we stumble and let giggles in.
Each mishap plays a funny tune,
Under the watch of a winking moon.

With friends to share our clumsy fate,
We roll in laughter and can't be late.
Life's little quirks, a comic spree,
In every fumble, joy sets free.

So here we are, twirling about,
With silly games leaving us in doubt.
Yet, through the mess, one thing is clear,
In every laugh, we conquer fear.

The Grinning Unknown

A riddle wrapped in joyful jest,
Life's a riddle that we bless.
With every twist, we giggle loud,
A mystery, yet we feel so proud.

In shadows deep, where giggles linger,
We chase the light with a pointed finger.
Questions float like balloons in air,
Defying gravity, free of care.

The unknown grins and winks at fate,
Enticing us to join the plate.
We juggle hopes like clownish dreams,
In a world bursting at the seams.

So let us leap, embrace the fall,
For in the jest, we find our call.
Through every doubt, we can't resist,
To find the joy in life's twist.

Snickers Amongst the Stars

Gazing up at the midnight sky,
A million winks pass us by.
Stars gossip in a silvery light,
In constellations of sheer delight.

They tell tales of cosmic pranks,
Of wandering dreams and filled-up tanks.
As planets dance in space so grand,
Our laughter echoes through the land.

On dreams' back, we ride and scream,
Through playful cosmos, we chase the dream.
In this expanse, we find our space,
With every smile, we leave a trace.

So let's toast to the silly night,
With giggles bright, everything feels right.
In the universe's quirky play,
We find our joy along the way.

Silly Serendipity

Life's a game of hopscotch,
We leap and sometimes fall,
Each step a funny moment,
Do we really know it all?

A cat on a sunny roof,
Chasing shadows with delight,
While we ponder grand designs,
She just wants to play all night.

Finding treasures in the dirt,
With giggles in our stride,
The daffodils are nodding,
As the clouds begin to glide.

So take your shoes off, dance free,
The world's a quirky spree,
In the mess of this puzzle,
Isn't that the key?

Giggling Through the Gauntlet

Running through the maze of life,
With a jester's cap in tow,
Chasing dreams like silly sprites,
With every laugh, we grow.

Dodging wisdom like a pro,
As we trip on all our schemes,
A tumble here, a giggle there,
Reality's just strings of dreams.

On this winding, jesting path,
We juggle thoughts and fears,
Each punchline is a stepping stone,
We'll laugh through all the years.

So grab a pie, take a slice,
Life's not meant to drudge,
In this playful masquerade,
We'll dance and laugh, no grudge!

The Irony of Infinite Questions

A question marks the shallow air,
Who needs a final quest?
With each 'why' we split our sides,
In confusion, we invest.

About the why and what and when,
We giggle and we squint,
The answers swirl like cotton candy,
In a world that likes to hint.

We ponder life's perplexing ways,
With a smirk upon our face,
In every doubt, a comic twist,
In this absurdity we embrace.

So here's a riddle wrapped in fun,
What's the point of all this fuss?
If the punchline is infinity,
ABCs and 1-2-3s, we trust!

Cosmic Shenanigans

Under the stars, a cosmic dance,
We twirl in joy and grace,
While aliens laugh at our concerns,
In this vast and silly space.

Planets giggle in their orbits,
While comets streak and play,
As we fumble through our seasons,
And add another 'maybe' day.

With each sunrise bringing giggles,
A rainbow in our eyes,
We trip upon reality's brink,
With wonder and surprise.

So let the universe jest with us,
In all its wild delight,
For every twist will bring a laugh,
As we revel in the night!

The Errant Laughter of Time

Tick tock, a jester's grin,
Making fools of what's within.
Chasing dreams that dance and sway,
Mirthful echoes lead the way.

In the mirror, ages frown,
Yet they wear a silly crown.
Riddles tossed like autumn leaves,
Life's a joke that never leaves.

Caught in yarns of daily strife,
Silly tales, this joyful life.
With every tick, a chuckle flies,
Finding fun 'neath serious skies.

So we sip our tea of glee,
On a whimsied, wobbly spree.
Time may tease, but we won't mind,
In this jest, the heart is blind.

Nonsense in the Narrative

A purple cow with polka dots,
Chasing dreams through tangled plots.
Waving flags of cotton candy,
Nonsense sweet and ever dandy.

A tale where fish ride bicycles,
And elephants wear icicles.
Every line, a merry twist,
Making sure we can't resist.

Silly stories lined with cheer,
Characters that disappear.
With every turn, the giggles grow,
In this wacky, whirling show.

So let's dance on silly peaks,
Where nonsense sings and laughter speaks.
In a world without a care,
Life's just one exuberant affair.

Whimsy in the Woven Web

Spiders weaving dreams of fun,
Caught in webs where jokes are spun.
A dance of colors, bright and bold,
Woven tales that never grow old.

A giggle here, a snicker there,
In the light, absurdities flare.
With every loop, a twist of fate,
Life's silly dance we celebrate.

Bouncing balls of jelly beans,
Floating boats on carpets, dreams.
Whimsy drapes the world in cheer,
Twirling truths we hold so dear.

Join the fun, let laughter flow,
In this web where joys bestow.
With every thread, a silly cheer,
In this fabric, life's sincere.

Guffaws Amidst the Chaos

In the crowd, a tumbleweed,
Chasing thoughts at lightning speed.
Chaos reigns, but we don't fret,
For laughter's song, we won't forget.

A cat that sings a lullaby,
While robots dance and chickens fly.
Underneath the cosmic play,
We find the joy, come what may.

Mismatched socks, a stylish trend,
Around each corner, giggles bend.
In chaos, bright and full of zest,
We learn to laugh—it's for the best.

So join the dance, embrace the fun,
Life's chaos under a glowing sun.
With every slip, and every twist,
Find the joy we can't resist.

www.ingramcontent.com/pod-product-compliance
Lightning Source LLC
Chambersburg PA
CBHW051655160426
43209CB00004B/907